RED DOG

This is a true story about a dog in Western Australia in the 1970s. There is a life-sized statue of him in the town of Dampier, put there by his friends after his death. People in the north-west still remember him, and tell stories about him . . . and smile.

Red Dog had many names. At different times he was called Tally Ho, Bluey, the Dog of the North-West, but mostly he was called Red Dog, or just Red. Everybody in the north-west knew Red. He never really belonged to anyone, but he had many friends. He was never without a place to sleep, or a good meal, before he moved on – because he was also a great traveller. It is a hard, hot country, up in the Pilbara region, but Red knew how to get around. He rode on buses and trucks, in people's cars, and on trains. If people saw Red Dog on the road, they always stopped and gave him a ride.

But there was one thing about Red Dog. You really, really didn't want to travel with him in a car with the windows closed . . .

OXFORD BOOKWORMS LIBRARY

True Stories

Red Dog

Stage 2 (700 headwords)

Series Editor: Jennifer Bassett
Founder Editor: Tricia Hedge
Activities Editors: Jennifer Bassett and Christine Lindop

AUTHOR'S NOTE

The real Red Dog was born in 1971, and died on 20th November 1979. The stories in this book are all based on what really happened to him, but the people in the stories are invented. This is because I know very little about the real people in Red Dog's life, and also because I would not like to give an untrue picture or make mistakes when writing about them. The only character in the story who is 'real' is John.

Louis de Bernières

LOUIS DE BERNIÈRES

Red Dog

Retold by
Jennifer Bassett

Illustrated by
Lachlan Creagh

OXFORD UNIVERSITY PRESS

OXFORD

UNIVERSITY PRESS

Great Clarendon Street, Oxford OX2 6DP

Oxford University Press is a department of the University of Oxford.
It furthers the University's objective of excellence in research, scholarship,
and education by publishing worldwide in

Oxford New York

Auckland Cape Town Dar es Salaam Hong Kong Karachi
Kuala Lumpur Madrid Melbourne Mexico City Nairobi
New Delhi Shanghai Taipei Toronto

With offices in

Argentina Austria Brazil Chile Czech Republic France Greece
Guatemala Hungary Italy Japan Poland Portugal Singapore
South Korea Switzerland Thailand Turkey Ukraine Vietnam

OXFORD and OXFORD ENGLISH are registered trade marks of
Oxford University Press in the UK and in certain other countries

ISBN: 978 0 19 479083 3

A complete recording of this Bookworms edition of
Red Dog is available in an audio CD pack ISBN 978 0 19 479045 1

Printed in China

ACKNOWLEDGEMENTS
*The Publishers are grateful to Louis de Bernières
for permission to adapt and simplify copyright text*

Word count (main text): 7,662 words

For more information on the Oxford Bookworms Library,
visit www.oup.com/bookworms

CONTENTS

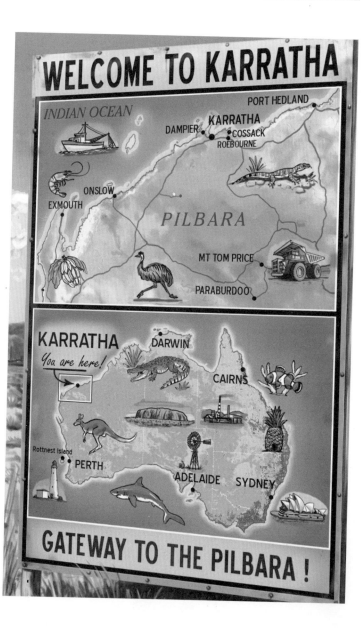

From Tally Ho to Red Dog

'Strewth!' said Jack Collins. 'He's done it again. It's a terrible smell – a real stink! How can that dog live with himself? When he breaks wind, I want to run out of the room.'

'Everyone likes their own smells,' said Mrs Collins.

'Oh yes?' said her husband. 'Well, it's too much for me, Maureen. Tally will have to live outside the house.'

'It's because of what he eats,' said Maureen. 'It's going to make smells. And he eats so fast too.'

'You know what?' Jack said. 'We'll give him to the army. They can send him to the enemy, and they'll all run, to get away from the stink.'

'Oh, he's done it again,' said Maureen, holding her nose. 'Tally, you're a bad dog.'

Tally Ho looked up at her with one yellow eye, and wagged his tail a few times. Her voice was friendly, and he thought that she was saying nice things about him. He closed his eye again, and went on thinking about food.

Tally Ho was only a year old, but already he was famous for eating. He ate everything. People gave him all kinds of things to eat – paper bags, sticks, small dead animals, apples, eggshells – and Tally Ho tried it all. He didn't like sticks much, but eggshells were all right, if they still had bits of egg inside. He ate the same food as the family ate too – meat and potatoes and vegetables.

'I'm going to take him out,' said Jack. 'He can have a run, and get some of that wind out.' He stood up and went to the door. 'Run time, Tally,' he said.

Tally began to jump up and down excitedly. The floor shook under his feet.

'Get him out before he shakes the place down,' said Maureen. Jack opened the door. Tally ran outside, and began to jump up and down by the car.

Jack opened the back door, and said, 'Jump in.'

Tally Ho jumped onto the back seat, then at once jumped over and sat in the front seat.

Jack opened the front passenger door. 'Out!' he said.

Tally looked at him, then looked away, and found something very interesting to watch down the street.

Jack didn't like this. He was an army man, and an order was an order. He picked Tally up, and moved him onto the back seat. 'Stay!' he said.

Tally waited. When the car was moving, he jumped into the front seat again. He put his head out of the open window. That way he couldn't hear any orders.

Jack shook his head. 'That dog just does what he wants,' he said. 'He thinks he's a person, I'm sure of it.'

At the airport Jack let Tally out of the car, and Tally ran the seven kilometres home, chasing the car through the hot afternoon, and loving every minute of it. When he arrived home, he drank about a litre of water, then went outside and lay down under a tree. That evening he ate 700 grams of dog food in just over ten seconds.

'That's one hungry dog!' said Jack.

When Tally was sure there was no more food, he went

Tally chased the car through the hot afternoon, loving every minute of it.

outside again. He had a little sleep, woke up, and thought about going walkabout, maybe chasing a wallaby. There were so many interesting smells out there in the dark! He got to his feet and set off into the night.

In the morning Jack Collins said, 'I think Tally's gone walkabout again.'

'One day he won't come back,' said Maureen.

'He always comes back in the end,' said her husband.

Three days later, Tally walked in, just in time for supper. His coat was dirty, his stomach was nice and full, and he looked very pleased with himself.

Maureen and Jack Collins had to move from Paraburdoo to Dampier. It was a long hot journey of about 350 kilometres, along a difficult road, full of holes.

They set off early before the sun got too hot. But after fifteen kilometres, Tally's stomach began to work on his breakfast, and a terrible stink filled the car. Then he broke wind again, even worse than before.

'Strewth!'

'Bad dog!'

Jack had to stop the car. He got out, pulled Tally out of the car, and put him into the trailer with all the chairs and tables and boxes.

'Sorry, mate, but if you can't hold it in, you're not coming with us. You'll have to ride in the trailer.'

Tally made himself comfortable between the legs of a

A terrible stink filled the car.

chair. He loved travelling from place to place, watching the world go by, seeing new places, making new friends.

In Dampier he lived with Jack and Maureen most of the time, but he often went walkabout for days at a time. One evening Jack took him out for a run on the beach.

There were lots of families there, having barbecues, and Tally soon got the wonderful rich smell of meat cooking over fires. Jack took hold of Tally's collar, to stop him running up to the barbecues. He didn't know any of the people on the beach, but to his great surprise, many people knew Tally.

'Look, there's Red Dog!' called one man.

Another man came and patted Red Dog on the head. 'Hello, Bluey, howya going? Welcome to the barbie.'

Soon Tally escaped from Jack's hold and ran away. A minute later Jack heard a cry.

'Hey! My steak – where is it? I put it down on my plate, and now it's gone!'

Then came a second shout. 'Who's taken my burgers?'

Jack hurried away. He knew Tally could find his way home, and he didn't want to talk to angry men about his dog stealing their dinners.

Red Dog, John, and Nancy

'I don't think he's coming back,' said Maureen. 'Yes, this time he's been away a long time,' Jack said, shaking his head.

They both knew that Tally was no longer their dog. He was moving on, spending more and more time away.

'He'll be all right,' said Jack. 'He knows how to find tucker. He never goes hungry, that's for sure.'

Tally found life too interesting to stay in one place. He always wanted to know what was going on round the next corner. He liked people, he liked Jack and Maureen, but he didn't love anybody. Sometimes a dog really loves somebody, and that person is their true friend. But Tally didn't have that one special friend.

It was lucky for him that Dampier was full of lonely men. There was a lot of building going on – new roads, a new railway, a new airport, new houses for the workers. And hundreds of men were now living in the town to do this work. They came from Poland, Italy, New Zealand, Ireland, Greece, England . . . and most of them had no wives or family with them. These hard, strong men liked Tally. It was good to have a dog to stroke, to have playfights with, to talk to – a dog who was always pleased to see you. Tally liked them, too. They played with him, they gave him food, they bought special meat for him. There was always a meal waiting for him when he came back from his travels.

No one knew his real name, and soon he was just called 'Red Dog', or just 'Red'. And Tally was in fact a red dog. He was a Red Cloud kelpie, a fine old Australian sheepdog, a very clever dog. He was a lovely dark red-brown colour, with golden-yellow eyes. His body was strong, and he was surprisingly heavy.

The men of the Hamersley Iron Company got to know Red Dog very well, because of John, one of their bus drivers.

John was half Maori, and people said that he was a friend to everyone. He was small, and young, and he loved animals more than anything. One day he was in Dampier, standing by his bus, waiting for his passengers, when he saw Red Dog in the street. He smiled, and went down on one knee, calling out, 'Hey, boy! Here!'

Red Dog stopped and looked at him.

'Come on, mate,' said John. 'Come and say g'day.'

Red Dog wagged his tail. He came over, and John took hold of his right paw and shook it.

'Pleased to meet you, mate,' he said. Then he took Red Dog's head in both hands and looked into his eyes.

'Hey, you're a beauty,' he said. And from that moment Red Dog knew that his life would be different.

When the men arrived to take their bus to work, they

'Hey, you're a beauty,' John said.

found John sitting in the driver's seat, and Red Dog sitting in the seat behind him. After that, Red Dog travelled everywhere on the Hamersley Iron buses, and he always had the seat behind the driver.

One day a stranger got on the bus. Nancy Grey was new in town. She was a secretary at Hamersley Iron, and she didn't know about Red Dog. The bus was full of workers, and there were no empty seats. There was just a seat behind the driver, which had a dog in it.

The men all sat there, watching and smiling. They wanted to see what would happen.

'Down!' said Nancy.

Red Dog looked up at her, then looked away again. He did not move, and showed that he had no plans to move out of *his* seat.

'Bad dog!' said Nancy, and Red Dog showed his teeth to her, just a little. Nancy was a bit surprised.

The men in the bus began to laugh at her. 'You'll never get him out of there,' said one man. 'That's his seat. No one sits there when Red wants it.'

Nancy did not like losing. She wanted to show these men and this dog that she wasn't going to run away. She sat down very carefully on the edge of Red Dog's seat. Red Dog showed his teeth again.

'Well, aren't you a nice friendly dog!' Nancy said.

'Well, aren't you a nice friendly dog!' Nancy said.

Showing teeth didn't make Nancy move, so Red Dog decided to push her off the seat. He put his nose under her leg, and pushed. But Nancy wasn't leaving now.

'I'm not moving,' she told the dog quietly, 'so you'll just have to sit next to me, and like it.'

Red Dog pushed again, and again, then decided to leave her sitting uncomfortably on the edge of the seat.

The next morning Nancy got on the bus, and again, there was Red Dog, sitting behind the driver's seat.

'Oh no,' thought Nancy. She now knew all about Red Dog from the people in the office. She sat down on his seat, a little closer than yesterday. Red Dog put his nose under her leg, and once again tried to push her off. But she wouldn't move. So Red Dog sat up, turned his back to her, and looked out of the window.

The next day Red Dog was waiting for Nancy to sit next to him, and he forgot to try to push her off the seat. And when Nancy said, 'Hi, Red!' and patted him on the head, he wagged his tail. But only once, and then he went back to looking out of the window. He didn't want to be too friendly, too quickly.

But from that moment, Red Dog and Nancy were friends. Not many people could sit next to Red Dog, but Nancy was one of them.

A night at the cinema

*T*here were not many unmarried women in Dampier in those days, so a lot of the men were interested in Nancy. John liked her too, and because Nancy sat with Red Dog in the seat behind the driver, he sometimes got to talk to her. One day Red Dog broke wind in the bus. The stink was terrible and everybody had to get out of the bus and wait for the smell to go. Red Dog wagged his tail, and walked around, being friendly with everyone.

John smiled at Nancy, and she smiled back. They both tried to stroke Red Dog at the same time, and their hands touched. They both laughed a little, and John said, 'Did you hear what happened yesterday on the bus?'

They began to tell Red Dog stories to one another, then after a time John said, 'There's a new film on at the Open Air cinema. Would you like to come and see it?'

'What is it?' asked Nancy.

'Can't remember,' said John. 'But they say it's good.'

'All right then,' said Nancy. 'We'll try it.'

That evening John cleaned his car, washed his hair, put on a new shirt . . . and tried to hide from Red Dog. This was difficult, because Red Dog loved him and followed him nearly all the time. But John didn't want Red Dog around on his night out with Nancy.

Everything was fine at first. He drove Nancy to the Open Air cinema at Karratha, opened the sunroof on the car, and the film began. It was a lovely warm evening, and the stars were bright in the sky above. John began to plan how to kiss Nancy. He put his arm around her, and waited for a good moment in the film. Nancy moved her head a little nearer to John's, and John put a small kiss on the side of her head. Things were going well. Then there was a sudden scratching noise on the car door.

'Oh no,' John said.

'What was that?' asked Nancy.

'It's Red,' said John. 'He's found us.'

There was a sudden scratching noise on the car door.

Red Dog scratched again, and John looked unhappy.

'Aren't you going to let him in?' asked Nancy.

'No. You know what he's like.'

'Oh, don't be unkind, John. Let him in.'

'He comes to see all the films,' said John. 'But why doesn't he sit with the people who brought him?'

'I'll let him in,' said Nancy. She opened the back door, and Red Dog jumped in, his tail wagging happily.

'Oh, Nance!' said John. 'Why did you do that?'

For a time, all was well. Red Dog watched the film, and John quietly put his arm around Nancy again. He gave the side of her head another little kiss, and at once Red Dog put his feet up on the back of the front seats, and pushed his head in between them.

Nancy laughed, and John said, 'Get down, Red, and be quiet!'

The love story in the film was getting interesting, and John decided it was a good moment for his first, real kiss with Nancy. But when he moved closer to her, the most terrible stink suddenly came from the back seat.

'Strewth!' said John, and Nancy opened the door and jumped out. 'Red,' said John, sounding tired, 'you really are a terrible dog.'

Red Dog looked pleased with himself, and John and Nancy never did have that kiss. John said that with Red Dog in his life, it wasn't possible to have a girlfriend.

An expensive day for a dog's friends

One morning Nancy telephoned the bus drivers' office at Hamersley Iron. 'Is John there?' she asked. 'It's really important.' Luckily, the men were having smoko, and John came to the phone at once.

'It's about Red,' said Nancy. 'Look, John, it's bad news. Somebody's shot him.'

'Someone's shot Red? What d'you mean, shot?'

'I found him, just now, when I was driving along the road near Seven Mile Creek,' Nancy said. 'My friend Patsy is with me, and she stayed with him while I came to phone. I'll get back there and wait for you, OK?'

John put down the phone. White-faced, worried, and angry, he turned to the other bus drivers. 'Where's the nearest vet?' he asked.

'Port Hedland,' said Jocko. He was from Scotland. No one knew his real name; everyone just called him Jocko.

'Strewth, that's four hours' drive,' said John. 'Red could die before we get there.'

'I'll come with you, mate,' said Jocko. 'I'll do the first aid.' Jocko was good at first aid.

'I'll come too,' said Giovanni, who was called Vanno.

'And me,' said Piotr, who was called Peeto.

John went to talk to their boss, who said they could

go. That was the good news. The bad news was that they would all lose a day's pay.

But they still wanted to go. Red Dog was special. He was John's dog, but he rode around on all their buses, and they all loved him.

They drove away fast in John's car, and at Seven Mile Creek they found Nancy and Patsy, and Red Dog. He was lying still at the side of the road. John put his hand on Red Dog's head. 'Hello, mate,' he said.

Red Dog was lying still at the side of the road.

Red Dog wagged his tail, just a little, at the sound of John's voice. He put his head on the ground. He felt tired, so tired, and his leg hurt like fire.

Jocko opened the first aid box, and got to work.

'There,' he said at last. 'He's lost a lot of blood, but I've stopped it now. Let's get him to the vet!'

'You drive, mate,' John said to Peeto. 'I'm going in the back with Red.'

Nancy and Patsy went home, and the four men set off for Port Hedland. While they drove, they talked about people who shoot dogs.

'I'd like to drive my bus over that man,' said Peeto.

'I'd like to hit him in the face,' said Jocko.

John just looked down at Red Dog, lying in his arms, and he said, 'Don't die, you terrible dog, don't die.'

After four hours' hard driving they arrived in Port Hedland, found the vet's place, and carried Red Dog inside. The vet told John to lay the dog on the table, and he began to look at the leg, now dark with dried blood.

'Nice first aid work,' said the vet. 'Who did that?'

'It was me, mate,' said Jocko, looking pleased.

'Will he be all right?' asked John.

'Too early to say,' said the vet. 'I'll have to get those bullets out.' He looked at the animal more closely, and said, 'Well, what d'you know? It's Red Dog, isn't it?'

'Strewth,' said Peeto. 'How did you know that?'

'Everyone knows this dog,' said the vet. 'The first time

I met him was at a barbie. Red Dog stole my burgers and four chicken legs. Everyone knows Red Dog. I think he's got some girlfriends around here, because I've seen some young dogs that look very like him.'

'Good boy,' said Jocko, patting Red Dog's head.

The men sat outside in the waiting room while the vet and his nurse took the bullets out of Red Dog's leg. It was a long, worrying time for them, but after half an hour the vet came out.

'I think he'll be fine,' he said. 'Lucky for him, the bullets didn't hit anything important. Give him some time to wake up, and we'll see how he is.'

They came back in a while, and found Red Dog not moving, but awake, and very pleased to see them.

'I need to keep him another hour or two,' said the vet. 'So why don't you all get something to eat?'

'Yes, I think it is tucker time,' said John.

The four men found a café, ate a big meal, and then decided to go for a drink. They felt happy – Red Dog was fine, and all was well. So they had a beer, and then another one, and another . . .

After an hour they went back to the vet's, ready to take Red Dog home. He was full of life, but the vet's bill was not good news. They looked at it unhappily.

'We haven't got this much money,' said Peeto.

'Could we pay you later?' asked John. 'The boys back home will help us out.'

The vet looked at their worried faces. 'OK,' he said. 'But you've had too many beers to drive home tonight.'

This was true, but they set off for home anyway. Somewhere near the Sherlock River bridge, a fast car came up behind them, with a blue light.

'Oh strewth,' said Peeto. 'It's the police.'

A fast car came up behind them, with a blue light.

'We'll help you pay the fine,' said Vanno, laughing.

Peeto stopped the car and got out. The policeman got out of his car and came up with his notebook.

'Hello, Bill,' said Peeto.

'I'm not Bill when I'm working, mate,' said the policeman, who lived in the same street as Peeto.

'And when you're working, I'm not "mate". I'm "sir",' said Peeto, smiling.

That was Peeto's big mistake. It is not a good plan to be clever with a traffic policeman when you are full of beer and driving a car.

The next day during smoko they worked out the cost of Red Dog's shooting. They lost a day's pay, there was the cost of petrol for the long drive, the cost of the meal and the beer, the vet's bill, and the police fine.

'Hey,' said Vanno unhappily. 'What say the next time we buy a plane and fly the vet in? It's gotta be cheaper than this.'

Where is John?

John bought a big motorbike because on hot days he liked riding around with the wind in his face. He tried putting Red Dog on the seat in front of him, but Red Dog preferred the comfortable seats of cars and buses. When John went out in his car, Red always wanted to go too, but when John got on his bike, Red stayed at home, or went visiting his friends to get a meal.

One night John went to have a meal at the house of some friends, and he took the bike. It was July, and the nights were very cold. Red Dog was out, looking for other dogs to fight, and wallabies to chase.

What happened that night will always be a mystery.

John had some beers, but not too many, and he left his friends after a happy evening and a good meal.

On the road coming into Dampier, there is a sudden bend, and on both sides of the road there are great red rocks. Perhaps John was going a bit too fast, perhaps there was something wrong with his bike, perhaps there was a stone on the road.

But something went wrong, and John hit the side of the road and went flying through the air. He came down on one of the great rocks. No one knows how long John lay dying. He tried to get back to the road, but he was too badly hurt. And after a while that kind, animal-loving man, who was a friend to everyone, died alone in the rocks by the road. Perhaps he thought about Red Dog while he slowly fell into that long last sleep, on that cold and starry night.

The next morning John did not come in to work, and his friends were worried.

'I got a bad feeling,' said Vanno, shaking his head.

'It's not like John,' said Peeto. 'He phones in if he's not coming.'

'Let's give him until smoko,' said Jocko, 'and if he's still not here by then, I'll go out and look for him.'

John was not there by breaktime, so Jocko went round to John's little house. He found Red Dog waiting outside the door. The dog got to his feet and wagged his tail.

'Where's your mate?' asked Jocko. He knocked on the door, but he knew there would be no answer. John never left Red outside if he was at home. John's car was there, but not his motorbike, and Jocko remembered about the dinner with friends. Jocko went back to the bus station and phoned the friends.

'When John left you last night, was he on his bike?'

'Yes. Why? What's up?'

'He never got home.'

Jocko borrowed a car and drove along the road from the friends' house. He was a motorbike rider himself, and he knew which places were dangerous for a bike rider.

'Where's your mate?' asked Jocko.

When he came to the bend near Dampier, he stopped the car and got out. He walked across the road, and looked down over the red rocks.

Dampier was a small place back then, and everyone knew John and liked him. His death made everyone unhappy. He was too young, much too young, to die so suddenly. He died with all his life in front of him, leaving behind some good friends, and a dog who loved him.

When someone dies, there is a lot to do. Three days later, someone remembered Red Dog, and found him still waiting outside John's house. John's friends brought food, and Red Dog ate it, then lay down again outside the door. He slept there through the cold nights, waiting, waiting, waiting . . . for John to come home.

After three weeks he went to the bus station, and spent half his time there with his friends the bus drivers, and half his time outside John's house. What goes on in a dog's head? No one knows how much language a dog has, or how they think. But there was surely one big question in Red Dog's head:

'Where is John?'

If you are a dog, and you lose your master, your one special friend, it is a terrible thing. Red Dog had only one plan. He went to every place that John knew, looking in every corner for him, hoping and hoping to find him.

From this time Red Dog became the Dog of the North-West. He belonged to everyone because he could never find John again, and there was no one who could take his place.

The Dog of the North-West

Red Dog had his greatest adventures after John's death. He always liked travelling, but when John was alive, Red Dog liked to be with him. Now he was free, and answered to nobody.

He was well known and well loved in the North-West, and every week somebody tried to give him a home, make him comfortable, give him good meals. Red Dog liked all these people, and he often stayed a while, but he always moved on sooner or later. Then, months later, there he was, scratching at the door, back again for a short visit and a good meal.

He travelled as usual on the Hamersley Iron buses, and in the train to Mount Tom Price. He watched people's faces carefully, still looking for John. He travelled 900 kilometres to Broome with a road train, and stayed for two weeks, eating every night at the town's hotel. He looked everywhere, but couldn't find John, so he came back in an old car with a large family.

One day he was outside Nancy's caravan on a terribly hot summer day. Nancy and Patsy, with another friend called Ellen, were getting ready to go on holiday. They were planning to drive to Perth, 1,500 kilometres to the south, where it was much less hot.

'Hello, Red,' said Patsy. 'Got nothing to do?'

'Why don't we take him with us?' said Ellen. 'He'll enjoy the ride.'

'Want to come to Perth?' asked Nancy. She patted the seat beside her, and the dog jumped into the back. Women smelled nice, and often gave you sweet things to eat, like chocolate. So Red Dog decided to go with them.

Red Dog enjoyed the many ball games on the beach.

The three women soon remembered why it was a mistake to travel with Red Dog in a small car. They spent the two days' drive saying, 'Pooee! Pooee!' and 'Oh no, not again, Red!' But Red Dog usually had his head out of the window, and so did not hear them.

Patsy, Ellen, and Nancy went swimming, and lay on the beach in the sunshine. Red Dog enjoyed swimming too, and also the many ball games on the beach. In one game he ran away with the ball, and people had to chase him up the beach to get it back.

One day Patsy said, 'Let's go to Rottnest tomorrow.'

'You can't take a dog over to Rottnest Island, can you?' said Nancy. 'What'll we do with Red?'

'Where is Red, anyway?' said Ellen, sitting up.

They looked up and down the beach, they called and shouted, they went to the hotels and cafés, they looked through the park. Red Dog was nowhere.

'You know what we've done?' said Patsy. 'We've lost the most famous dog in Western Australia.'

'When we get home, they're going to kill us,' said Nancy. 'What are we going to do?'

'Just think,' said Ellen unhappily, 'what Jocko and Peeto and Vanno will say.'

That was the end of their holiday. They went to the best fish restaurants, but they couldn't eat. They went shopping, but they couldn't find anything to buy. So they went home, worrying about Red Dog all the way.

When at last they got home, late at night, they found Red Dog waiting for them outside Patsy's caravan. He didn't like Perth very much, and he couldn't find John on the beach, so he found a truck-driver to give him a ride home. The three women were really pleased to see him, and gave him a big meal.

'But you're a bad boy, Red,' said Patsy. 'Look what you did to our holiday!'

'We've still got a few days holiday, so why don't we go down to Exmouth?' Nancy said.

'Yeah, why not?' said the other two. They all looked at Red Dog, and Ellen said, 'Are we taking Red?'

'Not on your life!' said Nancy and Patsy.

Red Dog went to visit Jocko, Peeto, and Vanno at Hamersley Iron, and then he went and stayed for a night at the Walkabout Hotel in Karratha. The cook there was a friend of his, and always gave him a good meal. Three days later he gave the three women a very great surprise when he walked past their café in Exmouth. He was pleased to see them, but by the next morning he was on his way to Onslow with another truck-driver friend.

Nancy, Patsy, and Ellen all lived in caravans in the caravan park. Many people were living there while they waited for the builders to finish the new houses. The park was a nice place, with flowers everywhere – but there were two things wrong with it.

One thing was a rule which said NO DOGS, and the other thing was a caretaker who liked rules, and who did not like dogs. His name was Mr Cribbage and every time he saw Red Dog, he tried to chase him away.

There was also a cat who lived in the caravan park, called Red Cat. He liked the rule about NO DOGS because he hated dogs. He was a big cat, with orange-red fur, green eyes, and great paws, which hid long, dangerous claws. Red Cat never lost a fight.

Red Cat also lived in the caravan park.

Red Dog liked chasing cats. He was a cleverer dog than most, but like most dogs he did not understand cats.

He met Red Cat one day behind Nancy's caravan. At once he jumped forward to begin the chase – and then stopped, because Red Cat did not run. He sat still, opened his mouth, and hissed. Red Dog jumped again, but still Red Cat did not run. He hissed again, even louder, and his fur stood up all along his back.

Red Dog began to feel less sure of himself, but he still wanted to chase. He tried again, but Red Cat hit out with his claws, and blood began to run from Red Dog's nose. Red Dog showed his teeth and growled. Red Cat showed his teeth and hissed. Nose to nose, growling and hissing, the two animals moved slowly round in a circle. Red Cat scratched Red Dog again. Red Dog tried to use his teeth, but was too slow. Then Nancy came round the corner and stopped the fight.

There was now a new vet in Roebourne, which was much nearer than Port Hedland, and Nancy took Red Dog there.

The young vet cleaned the scratches on Red Dog's nose, and said, 'I saw a dog just like this last week. But he had a different owner. And the week before, another man brought in a dog just like this. Why are there so many dogs round here that all look the same?'

Nancy smiled to herself. Red Dog was everybody's dog now, and when Red Dog needed to go to the vet, one of his many friends took him. One day soon the vet would understand the mystery.

When Red Dog went back to the caravan park, he looked for Red Cat. They began hissing and growling again, but the fight never happened. And one day people saw something very surprising. Red Dog and Red Cat were sitting together, side by side, watching the sun go down, just like two old people sitting in their garden.

They were strange friends, it's true, but friends they were. Red Cat still hated dogs, but not Red Dog. Red Dog still chased cats, but not Red Cat. One day Nancy took a picture of Red Dog sleeping, with Red Cat sleeping on top of him. She made two copies, sent one to a newspaper, and put the other copy on her wall.

Red Dog and his friends

During the years after John's death Red Dog travelled all over the North-West. He had many adventures and accidents, and made many new friends. Once he fell off a trailer and hurt his leg. A man called Don, who worked at Dampier Salt Company, found him and took him to the vet in Roebourne. The vet knew all about Red Dog now.

'He stayed with me once for a few days,' the vet told Don. 'Then he went off again. You know what he does? He knows which cars come from Dampier. So he looks for one, then goes and sits next to it until the driver comes back. Then he gets a ride back home.'

Vets cost money, of course, and who was going to pay the vet's bills for Red Dog? This is what the men of Dampier Salt Company did. They opened a bank account for him at the Wales Bank, under the name 'Red Dog', and everybody put a little money in.

He was a dog who belonged to everybody in that part of Australia, and he was often called 'The Dog of the North-West'. But he had a third name too. In Australia anyone with red hair is called 'Bluey', and some people called him that.

To Mr and Mrs Cribbage, Red Dog did not have a

name. He was just 'that dog'. Red Dog often visited his friends in the caravan park, and one day Mrs Cribbage saw him when he was scratching at Patsy's door.

She ran up to him, shouting, 'Hey, you! Off! Away!'

Red Dog looked at this strange fat woman, and scratched again on Patsy's door. Patsy opened the door.

'Hey, you! Off! Away!' shouted Mrs Cribbage.

'What's up?' she asked Mrs Cribbage.

'NO DOGS!' said Mrs Cribbage.

Patsy looked at her. 'You don't understand. This isn't just any dog. This is Red Dog.'

'A dog's a dog,' said Mrs Cribbage. 'It doesn't matter if it's the Queen of England's dog. This is a dog, and that's that. NO DOGS!'

'Red Dog's special,' Patsy said. 'Everyone knows that.'

'Get that dog out of here,' said Mrs Cribbage. 'I'm telling you. If you don't, we'll shoot it, and we'll get you and your caravan out of the park too.'

Mrs Cribbage walked away, feeling pleased. Rules were rules, and she and her husband were the bosses in this caravan park. The next day she and Mr Cribbage made a lot of new notices that said NO DOGS. They went round the park and put a notice up on every tree.

The people in the park shook their heads. They agreed a plan to stop Mr and Mrs Cribbage catching Red Dog.

'If anyone sees the Cribbages when Red Dog is visiting,' said Nancy, 'just shout "Cats" loudly. Then we'll hide Red Dog and the Cribbages won't see him.'

Mr and Mrs Cribbage never understood why people in the park went around shouting 'Cats' all the time.

Now, it happened that both Patsy and Nancy were afraid of the dark. And at night there were no lights in the park. So if they had to go out of their caravans to the dunny (that was the toilet), they didn't like it.

Red Dog could smell his way around in the dark, but he understood that Nancy and Patsy were afraid. It was a strange thing, but when they needed to go to the dunny at night, there was Red Dog. He walked with them to the dunny, and then walked back again to the caravan. He had lots of nice little meals to thank him for this.

But one night Mrs Cribbage came out of the dunny at the same time as Patsy . . . and saw Red Dog.

'What did I tell you about that dog?' she cried. 'You're out, girl! I told you. You'll have to leave this park!'

Patsy felt angry with the Cribbages and their stupid NO DOGS rule. 'Aw, get lost, why don't you?' she said.

'You wait!' shouted Mrs Cribbage. 'You just wait!'

Patsy turned and walked away. 'Come on, Red, let's go back to bed.'

The next morning somebody pushed a letter under her door. It said:

There is a rule in the park about dogs – NO DOGS. You are keeping a dog and we have told you not to, many times. You must now leave this park. Tomorrow morning at 9.30 we will take your caravan out.

Mr and Mrs Cribbage

Patsy went round to Nancy's. 'What am I going to do?' she said. 'Where am I going to live? This is terrible. They're taking my home away, just because of a dog!'

Nancy put her hand on Patsy's arm. 'Don't you worry,' she said. 'And don't start packing. I know what to do.' She took the letter and went from caravan to caravan, showing it to everyone.

The next morning, at 9.20, Mr Cribbage picked up the keys of his truck from the table.

'There's a lot of people driving around this morning,' said Mrs Cribbage, looking out of the window. 'What are they all doing?'

When Mr Cribbage went outside, he understood. There were cars everywhere – in a circle all around his truck, and across all the roads in the park. He couldn't go anywhere. Nobody could go anywhere.

He was too angry to speak. And what was worse, all the people in the park stood around, watching him, smiling, calling out:

'Going to take Patsy's caravan away, were you?'

'Want any help?'

'Looks a bit difficult to me.'

Mr Cribbage found his voice. 'That dog has to go. It doesn't belong to anyone. I'm calling the police.'

'That's no good,' someone shouted. 'Red's a friend of Bill's. And Red belongs to everybody.'

Mr Cribbage stood for a moment, then turned and went back into his office. He came out with a gun in his hands. He put two bullets into the gun, put the gun under his left arm, and patted it with his right hand.

'When I see that dog,' he called out, 'he's getting this.'

He turned round and went back inside.

Mr Cribbage came out with a gun in his hands.

Outside, things happened very quickly. 'He can't do that,' people said. 'He's mad! He can't shoot Red Dog.'

'I'm calling the RSPCA,' said Patsy.

'I'm calling the boys at Hamersley Iron,' said Nancy.

The RSPCA man arrived and told the Cribbages that

they couldn't just shoot a dog. Later, a yellow bus arrived from Hamersley Iron. The workers were strong, hard men, and they were tired after their day's work, tired and angry. They pushed into Mr Cribbage's office and all crowded around his desk. Jocko put his hands on the desk and looked down at Mr Cribbage.

'Now, are you the little piece of dirt that wants to shoot Red Dog?'

The next morning, very early, Patsy knocked on Nancy's caravan door. 'Nance – look! They've gone!'

It was true. The Cribbages were no longer there. Their caravan was gone, they were gone – everything was gone. No one ever saw them again.

'I feel terrible,' said Patsy, later. 'We've run them out of town. It's not a very nice thing to do, is it?'

'Too late now,' said Nancy. 'And who's sorry that they've gone?'

No one knows what Red Dog thought. He went looking for John one more time, riding all the way down to sweet Adelaide on a trailer. He came back two months later on a road train. By the time he next scratched on Nancy's door, there were new caretakers and new rules.

The last journey

For all of us there comes a time when our luck ends. Some of us die alone, and some not, but everyone goes alone through that last dark door at the end of life.

Red Dog was only eight years old, but he was getting tired. He rode all over Western Australia looking for John, he got into fights, sometimes he ate too much, sometimes too little. People shot at him, he fell off trucks and trailers; he was cold at night and too hot by day.

One day Nancy was brushing his coat when she found bullet holes in his ears. That was a lucky escape, but one Saturday in November Peeto was driving in his truck from Karratha to Dampier. He saw something dark red at the side of the road. He stopped and got out.

Red Dog was in convulsions. His legs, his head, – every part of his body was shaking, trying to break itself to bits. It was terrible to watch. Peeto tried to lift him into the truck, but he couldn't get a hold on him. Luckily, Bill the policeman came past, and stopped to help. People always stop to help when someone is in trouble on the road. Between them, they got him into the truck.

'What is it?' said Peeto. 'What's the matter with him?'

'It's poison,' said Bill. 'I've seen it before. They get these convulsions that last for hours, and then they die.'

They drove to the police station, and called the vet in Roebourne. But the vet was away, and not back until the next day.

'We can't let it go on like this,' said Peeto. 'Look at him, the poor old dog. It's terrible. We've got to stop it.'

'You're right,' said Bill, 'but I don't want to.'

'You've got to, mate,' said Peeto softly. 'If he goes on like this, he'll break all his bones.'

They carried Red Dog outside. The convulsions were still terrible, but Peeto held him down, and Bill put his gun to the dog's head. Birds sang in the trees above. Peeto closed his eyes, and waited. Nothing happened.

'I'm sorry,' said Bill. He put his gun down. 'I can't do it, I just can't do it.'

They called up all Red Dog's friends, and they came round to the little police station. One after another they held Red Dog while the convulsions went on, and they waited for the vet. They knew Red was dying. They drank tea, and told again all the stories about their old friend . . . the journeys . . . the terrible stink when he broke wind . . . finding him by their cars, asking for a ride . . . arriving at their doors, looking for a meal . . .

'Everyone's got a Red Dog story,' said Jocko. 'Someone must write them all down.'

The vet arrived the next morning. 'Yes, it's poison,' he said. 'But he's a strong dog. Let's try and save his life. Hold him down for me while I give him an injection.'

*They drank tea, and told again all the stories
about their old friend.*

He gave Red Dog an injection to stop the convulsions, and slowly Red Dog's body stopped shaking and lay still.

For two days Red Dog lay still, then he woke up, wagged his tail, and ate a meal. Everybody was so excited and happy.

But the vet had a bad feeling about it. A day or two later Red Dog began to walk into things, and fall down.

'It's no good,' the vet said. 'He can't see, and he can't walk. He's not himself. The light in his eyes has gone out. We tried, but now it's time to finish. I'm sorry.'

Patsy, Ellen, Nancy, Bill the policeman, and the boys from Hamersley Iron and Dampier Salt all called in to say goodbye. The men patted Red Dog on the head, they stroked his back, they pulled his ears. Silently they came in, and silently they went out, trying not to cry, because Aussie men are big strong men, and big strong Aussie men don't cry. The women kissed Red Dog on the top of his head, and they stroked his neck. They put their arms around him and held him, and they cried.

When everyone was gone, the vet said his goodbye to Red Dog too. He stroked Red Dog's head softly.

'Time to go, old mate, time to go.'

Then he did what he had to do.

Who knows what Red Dog thought about while he lay dying? Perhaps he remembered the good times – going walkabout, chasing wallabies, sitting with Red Cat in the caravan park, riding across the North-West in the trucks and trailers of his many friends. And perhaps in that last sleep, after years of looking, he found John again.

They buried Red Dog in stony red ground between Roebourne and Cossack. No one remembers the place now. His friends put up a monument to him in Dampier, and that is the only thing left of Red Dog. That, and the stories about him, and his collar with its tag, which on one side reads: *Red Dog – Bluey*, and on the other side: *I've been everywhere, mate.*

GLOSSARY

bank account people put their money into a bank account, and
the bank keeps the money safe for them

barbecue (barbie) a party outside, with food cooked on a fire

bend (*n*) a part of a road that is not straight

boss a person at work who tells other people what they must do

break wind to let gas out of the body through the bottom

bullet a small piece of metal that comes out of a gun

bury to put a dead body in the ground

caravan a kind of house on wheels that is pulled by a car; **caravan
park** a place where many caravans can be parked together

caretaker a person whose job is to look after a caravan park, etc.

chase to run behind somebody or something and try to catch it

claw one of the hard pointed parts on an animal's or a bird's foot

coat the hair or fur that covers an animal

collar a band that you put round the neck of a dog or a cat

convulsion a sudden shaking movement of the body that cannot
be stopped

fine (*n*) money that people must pay because they have done
something wrong

first aid medical help given to someone before a doctor arrives

fur soft thick hair that covers the bodies of some animals

g'day (*Australian English*) hello

growl (*v*) (of a dog) to make a low angry sound

hiss (*v*) to make a noise like a very long 's'

howya (*Australian English*) how are you

injection putting a drug into the body using a special needle

kiss (*v & n*) to touch someone with your lips to show love

Maori a member of a race of people who were the original
people living in New Zealand

mate (*informal*) a friend

monument something that is built to help people remember a person, an event, etc.

motorbike a vehicle with two wheels and an engine

order (*n*) words that tell somebody to do something

pat (*v*) to touch somebody or something lightly with your hand

paw an animal's foot

poison something that will kill you or make you ill if you eat it

RSPCA Royal Society for the Prevention of Cruelty to Animals

rule (*n*) something that tells you what you must or must not do

scratch (*v*) (of a dog, a cat) to move the claws across something

set off to start a journey

sheepdog a dog that is trained to help control sheep on a farm

smoko (*Australian English*) a tea-break (a time of rest at work)

steak a wide flat piece of meat (usually meat from a cow)

stink (*n*) a very bad smell

strewth (*Australian English*) a word used to express surprise, etc.

stroke (*v*) to move your hand gently over something to show love

trailer a container with wheels that a car pulls along

truck a big vehicle for carrying heavy things

tucker (*Australian English*) food

vet a doctor for animals

wag (*v*) (of a dog's tail) to move from side to side

walkabout (**to go walkabout**) (*Australian English*) disappearing into wild country to travel around and live off the land

wallaby an Australian animal like a small kangaroo

ACTIVITIES

Before Reading

1 **Read the back cover and the story introduction on the first page of the book. How much do you know now about the story? Tick one box for each sentence.**

	YES	NO
1 Red Dog lived in one place all his life.	☐	☐
2 Red Dog had more than one name.	☐	☐
3 The stories about Red Dog are all true.	☐	☐
4 Red Dog had one owner all his life.	☐	☐
5 Red Dog's friends often gave him a meal.	☐	☐
6 Everybody in the north-west knew Red.	☐	☐
7 There is a statue to him in Western Australia.	☐	☐
8 Red Dog is still alive.	☐	☐

2 **What will happen in the story, do you think? Make some guesses. For each sentence, circle Y (Yes) or N (No).**

1 Red Dog learns to hate people. Y / N
2 Red Dog has an accident and loses a leg. Y / N
3 Somebody shoots Red Dog and he nearly dies. Y / N
4 A bus-driver becomes Red Dog's special friend. Y / N
5 Red Dog lives for a great many years. Y / N

3 **Why do you think people didn't want to travel with Red Dog in a car with the windows closed?**

ACTIVITIES

After Reading

1 **What was Red Dog like? Here are some sentences about him, but not all of them are true. Choose the true sentences, and put them together to make a paragraph. Use *and* or *but*, and leave out any unnecessary words.**

1 Red Dog was a Red Cloud kelpie, an Australian sheepdog.
2 He loved travelling from place to place.
3 He loved riding on a motorbike.
4 He liked seeing new places.
5 He didn't like meeting new people.
6 He always knew how to find tucker.
7 He only ate one kind of meat.
8 His many friends often gave him meals.
9 Sometimes he stole meat from barbecues.
10 John was Red's special friend, and Red loved him.
11 After John's death, Red forgot about him.
12 After John died, Red looked for him everywhere.
13 Red liked going walkabout.
14 He liked chasing wallabies and cats.
15 He never chased Red Cat.
16 He was famous because of the stink when he broke wind.
17 He was famous because he travelled all over Western Australia.

2 **Use these words to complete these short passages (one word for each gap).**

barbecue, bullets, burgers, caravan, chase, circle, claws, like, park, push, seat, show, strong, teach, teeth, truck

1 'This new girl, Nancy, gets on the bus and sits down on the _____ behind the driver, where Red always sits. Red didn't _____ that at all! First he shows his _____ and then he tries to _____ her off the seat. We were all laughing.'

2 'It was difficult getting the _____ out, but luckily they didn't hit anything important. He's a _____ dog, and I think he'll be fine. Next week he'll probably be at a _____, stealing somebody's _____ and eating them!'

3 'Here's that dog again, visiting people in the caravans. I don't like it. This is my _____, and I live here. He'll try and _____ me, like all dogs do. When he does, I'll use my _____ on his nose. That'll _____ him a lesson . . .'

4 'Don't worry, I know what to do. I'll _____ this letter to everyone, and tomorrow morning everyone will drive their cars and park in a _____ around Mr Cribbage's _____. Then he won't be able to pull your _____ away.'

3 **In the passages above, who is speaking or thinking? Choose one person for each passage from the names below.**

Mrs Cribbage / a worker at Hamersley Iron / Patsy / Nancy / the vet at Roebourne / the vet at Port Hedland / Red Cat

4 Use the clues below to help you complete this crossword. Then find the hidden word in the crossword.

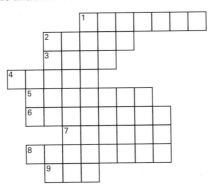

1 A _____ is an Australian animal.

2 Red Dog liked to _____ cats.

3 There was a _____ in the caravan park which said NO DOGS.

4 When Red Dog broke wind, there was always a terrible _____.

5 Nancy lived in a _____ while the builders were finishing the new homes.

6 At a _____, people often cook meat over an open fire.

7 Red Dog wore a _____ round his neck with his name on it.

8 Red's friends put up a _____ to him in Dampier.

9 When someone shot Red, his friends took him to the _____ in Port Hedland.

The hidden word in the crossword is _____.

5 **When Red Dog was having convulsions, Peeto called Red's friends. This conversation between Peeto and Jocko is in the wrong order. Put it into the right order and write in the speakers' names. Peeto speaks first (number 3).**

1 _____ 'Bill tried to, but he couldn't – he just couldn't do it. We'll have to hold Red down until he dies.'

2 _____ 'How bad is he? What does the vet say?'

3 _____ 'Hey, Jocko. Got some really bad news. It's Red.'

4 _____ 'I'm on my way. You get back to Red.'

5 _____ 'The vet's away. But Red's bad – he's having terrible convulsions. Bill thinks he's going to die.'

6 _____ 'Red? Why, what's happened?'

7 _____ 'No, I'll call them now. Get here quick, Jocko.'

8 _____ 'If Red's in real pain, you'll have to shoot him.'

9 _____ 'I found him on the road. He's eaten poison.'

10 _____ 'OK, I'll bring the boys with me. Have you called Nancy and Patsy?'

6 **What did you think about this story? Complete these sentences in your own words.**

1 I liked this story because _____.

2 The person I liked best in this story was _____ because _____.

3 For me, the funniest moment in the story was when _____.

4 For me, the saddest moment in the story was when _____.

ABOUT THE AUTHOR

Louis de Bernières was born in London in 1954, and now lives in Norfolk, in the east of England. He has university degrees in philosophy and education, and before he became a full-time writer, he worked as a gardener, a motorcycle messenger, and a car mechanic. He also taught English in Colombia in South America for two years.

De Bernières' first novel was published in 1990, and in 1993 he was selected by *Granta* magazine as one of the twenty Best of Young British Novelists. His international bestseller, *Captain Corelli's Mandolin*, won the Commonwealth Writers Prize in 1995, and was later made into a film. Many of his other novels have also won awards or been shortlisted for awards.

In an interview for an Americanonline magazine, de Bernières talked about his love of books and reading, and said, 'My mother or father used to read to me at bedtime, so I got into the habit of liking stories when I was very young and I think that there was never a time, almost, that I couldn't read.'

When he is not writing, Louis de Bernières enjoys gardening and repairing old cars. He plays the flute, mandolin, clarinet, and guitar, and performs regularly with the Antonius Players.

Red Dog was published in 2001. While visiting Western Australia in 1998, de Bernières saw the statue to Red Dog in the town of Dampier, and wanted to learn more about this wonderful dog. So he drove around collecting Red Dog stories, visiting the places that Red Dog knew, and writing a book about him. People all over the world have enjoyed the book.

'I hope,' Louis de Bernières has written, 'that my cat never finds out that I have written a story to celebrate the life of a dog.'

Here is a list of titles by Louis de Bernières:

   The War of Don Emmanuel's Nether Parts
   Señor Vivo and the Coca Lord
   The Troublesome Offspring of Cardinal Guzman
   Captain Corelli's Mandolin
   Sunday Morning at the Centre of the World (a play)
   Red Dog
   Birds Without Wings
   A Partisan's Daughter
   Notwithstanding: Stories from an English Village

OXFORD BOOKWORMS LIBRARY

Classics • Crime & Mystery • Factfiles • Fantasy & Horror
Human Interest • Playscripts • Thriller & Adventure
True Stories • World Stories

The OXFORD BOOKWORMS LIBRARY provides enjoyable reading in English, with a wide range of classic and modern fiction, non-fiction, and plays. It includes original and adapted texts in seven carefully graded language stages, which take learners from beginner to advanced level. An overview is given on the next pages.

All Stage 1 titles are available as audio recordings, as well as over eighty other titles from Starter to Stage 6. All Starters and many titles at Stages 1 to 4 are specially recommended for younger learners. Every Bookworm is illustrated, and Starters and Factfiles have full-colour illustrations.

The OXFORD BOOKWORMS LIBRARY also offers extensive support. Each book contains an introduction to the story, notes about the author, a glossary, and activities. Additional resources include tests and worksheets, and answers for these and for the activities in the books. There is advice on running a class library, using audio recordings, and the many ways of using Oxford Bookworms in reading programmes. Resource materials are available on the website <www.oup.com/bookworms>.

The *Oxford Bookworms Collection* is a series for advanced learners. It consists of volumes of short stories by well-known authors, both classic and modern. Texts are not abridged or adapted in any way, but carefully selected to be accessible to the advanced student.

You can find details and a full list of titles in the *Oxford Bookworms Library Catalogue* and *Oxford English Language Teaching Catalogues*, and on the website <www.oup.com/bookworms>.

THE OXFORD BOOKWORMS LIBRARY
GRADING AND SAMPLE EXTRACTS

STARTER • 250 HEADWORDS

present simple – present continuous – imperative –
can/cannot, must – *going to* (future) – simple gerunds …

Her phone is ringing – but where is it?

Sally gets out of bed and looks in her bag. No phone. She looks under the bed. No phone. Then she looks behind the door. There is her phone. Sally picks up her phone and answers it. *Sally's Phone*

STAGE 1 • 400 HEADWORDS

… past simple – coordination with *and, but, or* –
subordination with *before, after, when, because, so* …

I knew him in Persia. He was a famous builder and I worked with him there. For a time I was his friend, but not for long. When he came to Paris, I came after him – I wanted to watch him. He was a very clever, very dangerous man. *The Phantom of the Opera*

STAGE 2 • 700 HEADWORDS

… present perfect – *will* (future) – *(don't) have to, must not, could* –
comparison of adjectives – simple *if* clauses – past continuous –
tag questions – *ask/tell* + infinitive …

While I was writing these words in my diary, I decided what to do. I must try to escape. I shall try to get down the wall outside. The window is high above the ground, but I have to try. I shall take some of the gold with me – if I escape, perhaps it will be helpful later. *Dracula*

STAGE 3 • 1000 HEADWORDS
... should, may – present perfect continuous – *used to* – past perfect –
causative – relative clauses – indirect statements ...

Of course, it was most important that no one should see
Colin, Mary, or Dickon entering the secret garden. So Colin
gave orders to the gardeners that they must all keep away
from that part of the garden in future. *The Secret Garden*

STAGE 4 • 1400 HEADWORDS
... past perfect continuous – passive (simple forms) –
would conditional clauses – indirect questions –
relatives with *where/when* – gerunds after prepositions/phrases ...

I was glad. Now Hyde could not show his face to the world
again. If he did, every honest man in London would be
proud to report him to the police. *Dr Jekyll and Mr Hyde*

STAGE 5 • 1800 HEADWORDS
... future continuous – future perfect –
passive (modals, continuous forms) –
would have conditional clauses – modals + perfect infinitive ...

If he had spoken Estella's name, I would have hit him. I was so
angry with him, and so depressed about my future, that I could
not eat the breakfast. Instead I went straight to the old house.
Great Expectations

STAGE 6 • 2500 HEADWORDS
... passive (infinitives, gerunds) – advanced modal meanings –
clauses of concession, condition

When I stepped up to the piano, I was confident. It was as if
I knew that the prodigy side of me really did exist. And when I
started to play, I was so caught up in how lovely I looked that I
didn't worry how I would sound. *The Joy Luck Club*

BOOKWORMS · HUMAN INTEREST · STAGE 2

A Stranger at Green Knowe

LUCY M. BOSTON

Retold by Diane Mowat

When Ping sees Hanno in the zoo, he is excited, but also unhappy. Hanno is a magnificent African gorilla, big and black and much stronger than a man. But how can this wonderful wild animal live in a cage, behind bars and locked doors?

Then Hanno escapes from the zoo. And a few days later his footprints are seen near Green Knowe, the old house deep in the English countryside where Ping is spending his holiday . . .

BOOKWORMS · CLASSICS · STAGE 3

The Call of the Wild

JACK LONDON

Retold by Nick Bullard

When men find gold in the frozen north of Canada, they need dogs – big, strong dogs to pull the sledges on the long journeys to and from the gold mines.

Buck is stolen from his home in the south and sold as a sledge-dog. He has to learn a new way of life – how to work in harness, how to stay alive in the ice and the snow . . . and how to fight. Because when a dog falls down in a fight, he never gets up again.